AvonVoyage

A delightful and
informative companion
book to the
HTV series

AvonVoyage

Written
and illustrated by
Bob Baker

Absolute Press

Published by Absolute Press (publishers)
14 Widcombe Crescent, Bath, Avon. BA2 6AH

Published September 1982

© Bob Baker

ISBN 0 9506785 5 4

Design
Carl Willson MSIAD

Photographs
Charles Boulton

Cover printed by
Doveton Press, Rose Street, Bristol

Text photoset and printed by
Photobooks (Bristol) Ltd., Barton Manor,
St. Philips, Bristol

Bound by
The Pitman Press, Bath

To Bert Roach King Kong of Hotwells,
Tom Aliband who got me thinking,
and my gorgeous typist

Introduction

On the M4 motorway, somewhere between Chippenham and Swindon, is a sign which reads, 'River Avon'. It stands on a bridge taking the motorway over a fairly narrow stream. The sign made me wonder whether this Avon was in fact the Bristol Avon. Avon is quite a common English river name (from the Celtic word for water, *afon*). On returning, a look at the map assured me that it was indeed the Bristol Avon, way out there in the wilds of Wiltshire. I determined that one day I would travel the length of the Avon right up to the source. The opportunity to do this came some several years later when I suggested a travelogue/documentary about the Avon to HTV. In order to research the project I made an adventurous treck on cycle and on foot from the mouth to the source, accompanied by the intrepid Norman Bowler. It proved to be as exciting as I had hoped but totally exhausting, so on filming itself we chose to travel as far as possible by boats of various types, ending with Norman splashing his way on foot to the source.

It is my hope that the television series and the Avon Voyage book will help stimulate interest in the river which flows through the region. I have tried to show what the river can offer in terms of leisure and pleasure whether it be in pastoral countryside or busy city. I hope that some of the river's amazing history will promote further reading and investigation. I want readers to enjoy the Bristol Avon as much as I did. Happy hunting.

N.B. This book has been carefully designed to fit extremely large pockets.

Foreword

When I was first approached by HTV to front their new documentary series, 'Avon Voyage', my first reaction was to say politely, no. I'm an actor and the documentary was not my usual field, although it was something I had always wanted to try. After all, the documentary is an essential and important part of television.

So why not? – If I was going to be paid for having a lovely time on the River Avon, something that I have often done for my own pleasure, I would have a go.

Living in Bristol, I had often spent time on the river yet knew very little about the history or true nature of the place. In many ways it was not the easy trip I had visualised and I quickly learnt that it had nothing to do with being an actor, but it was a rich three weeks and I learnt a great deal.

We started filming in late summer 1981 from the mouth of the Avon aboard Tony Thomas's 'Sonia'. With us was Bert Roach, a lovely old character who has worked on the river for most of his life and used to have the grand title of 'licensed scavenger'. I had known Bert from around the local pubs in the Cumberland Basin for a number of years, so it was an easy and enlightening interview. Later on it became apparent that interviewers are only as good as the person that they are interviewing and I realised that not all could talk as fluently and as colourfully as Bert.

As we boated, punted, rowed and sometimes cycled along the Avon, I realised how little I really knew about the river and the docks which I had been overlooking all these years. What particularly surprised me was the tremendous variety to be discovered along its banks; the ingenious engineering feats which cope with the huge drop in tides, (the second highest in the world); the richness of its history; how the ships were built bigger and thus could not negotiate the notorious Horseshoe Bend and the eventual decline and fall of Bristol from the major port in England – 'when you could cross the Cumberland Basin from side to side walking on the decks of the ships' – to its present leisure boating and small ship building status.

Leaving Bristol through Netham lock we passed the large, sad and now extinct board mills, then suddenly and miraculously we came into the lush, green and gentle countryside. We had broken into a whole new world, interspersed only with small hamlets and good pubs, an occasional marina and Fry's Chocolate factory at Keynsham. And then the magnificent city of Bath! And what better way to arrive than by its river. Punting under the Pulteney Bridge one could sense the decadent pleasure of Beau Nash's eighteenth century – a time to be born rich and healthy, judging from the sort of health cures available at the time.

Outside Bath a visit to the Claverton pumping station with its huge dripping wheels slowly turning, giving us an insight into the power that was needed to pump the water up into the Kennet and Avon canal. Though no male chauvinist am I, it gave me great pleasure to be rowed very speedily and skilfully up river by the Bathampton Ladies Rowing Club to my next destination, and all I had to do was to simply shout out the occasional 'pull', a reversal of roles greatly appreciated.

And then to Luckington to find the source, but alas we found three! No doubt there are many more claims we did not find, but 'better to journey than to arrive' as they say and this journey was certainly rich in discovery. As for the source, well, we can only leave that to the local farmers to argue over as they discuss our Avon Voyage.

Norman Bowler

ISLE D'AVON. PORTAVON MARINA KEYNSHAM.

The Tidal Avon

Before the Bristol Port and Channel Dock Company decided to build a new dock at Avonmouth in the late 19th century, there was a small island at the mouth of the River Avon called Dunball Island, which, according to a certain Pill Hobbler, had a pub on it!

Avonmouth docks now stand on the northern bank and Portbury on the south. Here the mouth appears to be some three hundred yards wide. However, this is deceiving, because at high tide the water covers an extensive mud bank on the Portbury side. The deep water channel hugs close to the Northavon shore and winds in an 'S' bend, called the Swash Channel, before straightening again to continue on towards Bristol.

Just beyond the Avonmouth dock complex the Avon passes under the M5 bridge, an elegant box-girder structure. Fifty yards beyond the bridge, on the Portbury side, is an insignificant trickle of water falling into the Avon. It is called Morgan's Pill. This, but for a few financial problems, might have been the entrance of a Bristol to Taunton Canal. In the 1790's, during what was called "Canal Mania", a scheme was proposed to dig a canal from Morgan's Pill to Taunton, roughly following the line of the Bristol Channel as far as Bridgwater. In these days of powered ships this might sound a little crazy, but in the late 18th century a canal might well have competed with sailing ships, because on a canal there are none of the vagueries of wind and tide to worry about – things just keep moving.

The next pill to run into the Avon is Crockern Pill. The village which surrounds it is known simply as Pill, famous for its pilots, their boats (the pilot cutters) and its pubs. There were once more public houses than private dwellings. In its heyday Pill was a place of character, looking like a Cornish village with steep cobbled streets and whitewashed cottages, and still would be but for the fact that during the 1950's a Somerset County Council planner took Pill by the throat and shook all the character from the village. The little cottages were replaced by 'modern' apartments that look as if they should have been dismantled along with the Festival of Britain. Pill was a village of close-knit families of pilots, hobblers and boatbuilders. The pilots were a tough bunch of characters, who sometimes were forced to venture as far as one hundred miles west of Ireland 'seeking' ships to pilot up the Bristol Channel – such was the competition from Cardiff, Barry and Newport pilots. Their boats were usually built at Pill – the Bristol Pilot Cutters. There were half a dozen or so builders on the river at Pill. Famous names like the Morgans, the Coopers, the Prices and the Rowles. Names that are now part of boat building folklore. There is nothing left of this industry now, although it is possible to discern Rowles Slip, next to the old customs house on the Ham Green bank. What is a Hobbler? I once asked a Bristol dock gate man. He thought for a while and then answered – "Well they used to hobble the boats up, didn't 'um". "Thank you" I said. The answer seems to be that back in the days of sail the Hobblers of Pill would haul ships up the Avon to Bristol, either towing them by rowing boat or hauling them from the tow path by horses or even teams of men. With the introduction of powered ships, the Hobblers became Bristol River Pilots. They literally took charge of a ship from Pill to Bristol. Now that the Bristol City docks have virtually closed, the Hobblers take the lines from ships in the lock gate at Avonmouth.

A little further on from Pill is Hung Road where rather

Pill seen from Shirehampton – the remnants of Rowles slip can just be seen on the left of the picture

sinister black rocks jut out from the shore. The name, which has no connection with gibbets, derives from the fact that some sailing vessels disgorged their cargoes into lighters at this point and, to keep their vessels upright at low tide, the seamen would take a line from their masts to the shore and were thus 'hung' to the shore. Also in Hung Road is the Adam and Eve light with its little stone carving in-between the lights. An old story says that the towers were built by an outraged father in order to imprison his daughter and her lover, so that they could see each other but never, ever be together.

Staying on this shore, the rocky outcrops of Hung Road end at Chapel Pill in which quite a few sailing boats are now moored. I have no doubts whatsoever that the local yachtsmen would love to see this location exploited further. A mooring there would make a day's sailing in the Channel a real possibility.

Moving on up river, on the north bank at Shirehampton, is a rather strange looking, whitewashed building with a kind of bell tower. This is the powder house. Ships carrying gunpowder were made to offload it here so as to forestall any possibility of an explosion in the crowded city docks.

Just beyond the powder house is the notorious horseshoe bend. It was this purely natural phenomenon, more than anything, which finished Bristol as a port, for, as ships became bigger with the introduction of steam, the larger, more profitable ships, could not negotiate the horseshoe bend and so trade went elsewhere. Why a cutting was not made to eliminate this sharp bend is very hard to understand. Plans for such a cutting did exist and were still a matter of discussion by the City Council in the early seventies!

From the horseshoe bend the Avon straightens up before entering the gorge. Here the river is joined by, on the south bank, the Bristol to West Dock Freight Railway Line, and on the north bank, the Bristol to Avonmouth Line.

At Sea Mills the railway bridges the River Trym and the entrance to the oldest dock on the Avon. Roman in fact. Sea Mills dock, which the Romans called Abonae, used to transport lead, mined in the Mendips. It was connected by Roman road to Bath. Legend says that St. Patrick set sail to Ireland from Abonae. After Roman times Sea Mills, as a port, was overshadowed by Bristol, but, as the crumbling dock walls testify, the port was in use and in the eighteenth century became a floating dock – only the third to be built in England. Even so, Sea Mills was eventually abandoned as a port owing to the small size of its harbour.

Beyond Sea Mills the river flows through the Avon Gorge, a vastly imposing valley formed during the Ice Age, though not left untouched by man. The bare stone cliffs of the Gorge, now a haven for rock climbers, were created by quarrying during the 18th and 19th centuries. In the days before geology and natural history, in an effort to explain the origin of this Gargantuan gorge, a legend was created. It goes like this . . .

There were once two giants, brothers called Vincent and Goram and they were huge. "They'd have nursed the Colossus of Rhodes as a doll". The story goes that Vincent hacked out the Avon Gorge just for the hell of it, while the lazy Goram looked on. When Vincent had finished it, Goram decided that he must build a rival gorge. He was too lazy to provide his own axe, so he arranged with Vincent that he should throw HIS axe the three miles to where Goram was working on the River Trym. The arrangement worked perfectly until, by mistake, Vincent threw his axe and split Goram's head in two. Vincent's remorse was terrible. He felt that the best way to get over his grief would be to work and work, and so, in the words of an old rhymer:–

"He hewed himself a great armchair,
wherin he might sit with an easy air,
with such a view it was he who threw
the stones together at Stanton Drew,
and ranged in rank on Salisbury Plain
those wondrous piles that yet remain."

On the south bank just after Sea Mills is the Miles Dock, with just enough room for one barge. This dock was used for landing stone to build Leigh Court, completed in 1814. During the 1890's the dock was used again for loading celestine mined from Leigh Woods quarries – celestine is a mineral used in the pyrotechnics industry for fireworks, flares and distress rockets.

Before the Portway road was built, the Port and Pier Railway operated a service between Hotwells and Avonmouth. All that remains of this line are two tunnels through the limestone rocks, each side of Bridge Valley Road. The line was travelled by many a Bristol docker who had moved 'down the mouff', as they put it. In the early twenties a return to Avonmouth cost 8d! During the second world war a use was found for the Port & Pier's trackless tunnels – it stored pieces from the Bristol Museum and Art Gallery to save them from possible destruction by bombing.

Another defunct railway in the gorge, the Clifton Rocks Railway, ran from Hotwells to Clifton, where the terminal is still in existence beneath a roofing by the side of the Avon Gorge Hotel. At the Portway end you can see the pillars over the railway entrance, but unfortunately the whole structure has been filled in with brickwork. Also, here at the Rocks Railway entrance, is one of the Hotwells Spa water taps, the only one surviving.

Hotwells is the home of Bert Roach. *"They called my Granfer fishy. They called my old dad Roachy, but they calls me Mister Roach"*. Bert is self-styled King Kong of Hotwells. He was in his element in the thirties and forties when Hotwells was as rough a seaport as any in the world. After the war he became a licensed boatman on the river. This meant he could scavenge anything from the river, such as the occasional salmon stranded on the mud. This often brought him into conflict with other boatmen, looking for the same kind of windfall, notably the lads from Pill, who sometimes led him on a wildgoose chase by planting imitation paper 'salmon' on the mud. They used to watch from hiding as Bert struggled through the filthy mud only to find that he'd been tricked. This caused great mirth amongst the lads from Pill. Bert chose to beat them in his own way by going down the river at dead-low-water

What remains of the Clifton Rocks Railway on Hotwells Road

in the middle of the night. Amazingly enough the fish, if there were any, were just as easily spotted in darkness as in the daylight. The scales shone out under the moonlight. However being a boatman had its sombre side. They were expected, for a small fee, to retrieve bodies from the river mostly suicides from the Suspension Bridge. It seems that the pay was better if the corpse was delivered direct to the Somerset Bank.

The Avon Gorge is topped-off with a famous flourish. Isambard Kingdom Brunel's stately suspension bridge gracing the seaward entrance to Bristol. Decisions on the final design were long and tortuous. Originally it was a group of Bristol merchants who decided that there should be a bridge across the Avon Gorge. It was to be a showpiece for the City of Bristol. In 1753 William Vick, a wine merchant, donated £1,000 to the Merchant Venturers to start financing the Avon Bridge scheme. By 1829, as a result of shrewd investment, the sum had reached £8,000. Designs for the proposed bridge came flooding in to the Bridge Committee. One notable design was, believe it or not, Mr. Bridge's bridge. Described as "*A single immense arch of stone, 220 feet high and 180 feet span, carrying a 50 foot roadway . . . Immense abutments, carrying twenty dwelling houses, a lighthouse, toll house, chapel, granaries, a watermill, cotton and wool factories, a marine school, a library, a museum and subscription room, vertical windmills, a watch-house, out-offices, stablings, clock turret and belfrey . . .*" Plus a few other things!

Other designs were less grandiose. Telford's was felt to be rather safe and dated, two massive piers, à la Anglesey, supporting a suspension bridge.

The winning design was by Isambard Kingdom Brunel. His original design proved too expensive, so a "cut down" version was decided upon. Even then the money ran out before it was completed. The two bridgeless towers faced each other for years. It was finally completed after Brunel's death, using second-hand chains from the Hungerford Bridge in London.

The best way to see the gorge is, of course, by boat. The 'Tower Belle' makes the trip once a week in summer, a leisurely journey with a commentary by the skipper. Another way to enjoy the gorge is to walk or cycle down the recently completed tow-path cycle track. The track starts at the bottom of Rownham Hill and, allegedly, goes all the way to Pill, although, in reality, the track seems to peter out at Ham Green.

As the river enters the City of Bristol at Hotwells there is a junction. The Avon divides into a tidal section and the non-tidal floating harbour, which is entered by the lock gates at Hotwells. The entrance locks were built in the 19th century and have obscured the true course of the Avon. Before any dock construction the Avon followed the course of the present floating harbour and flowed out near the Long Ashton swing bridge, joining the present course. In 1981 the road and railway line at the junction of Cumberland Road and Avon Crescent subsided. This collapse was pretty well on the course the river used to take.

The tidal river beyond here is called the Cut – or the new course of the Avon. In order to make Bristol Docks into a floating harbour, the Avon had to be diverted. William Jessop, the engineer who created the new floating dock, chose a two-mile stretch from Temple Meads to Rownham. Making the Cut was no easy task since it had to go through hard sandstone, and many technical innovations were used, including steam pumps and tramways. There is a persistent myth in Bristol that the Cut was dug by French prisoners of war. This is not so.

The labourers were mainly Irish, who had previously worked on canals and railways.

The New Cut has a variety of bridges. Firstly the Ashton Swing Bridge; a double deck road and railway bridge until the new flyover at Cumberland Basin was built. The road section has now been removed. The bridge was built in 1906. The swinging section is 202 feet long but no longer swings. The lower rail section is still in use. The south bank of the New Cut is raised higher than the north bank. This is because, when digging the Cut, the spoil was tipped on that side. The sandstone which was removed during excavation was put to good use, and may still be seen in the floating harbour. It was used to build up the dock walls.

The next bridge is the Vauxhall Footbridge, opened in 1900, another non-swinging swing bridge. After a long straight, the New Cut passes the remains of Bristol Gaol, destroyed by fire in those other Bristol riots of the last century. Only the forbidding gate tower remains. Next to the gaol is the Wapping suspension footbridge. Just beyond this is the second entrance to the floating harbour, the lock gates and swing bridge of the Bathurst Basin, now completely redeveloped and looking very smart. The Bathurst Locks were sealed and the bridge, fixed in the early thirties, was closed because the volume of traffic fell.

Here the Cut turns and heads towards Totterdown, beneath Bedminster Bridge. This was originally a Jessop Bridge, built in 1807, but it was rebuilt in 1884, widened, and then duplicated as motor traffic increased in the fifties.

Beyond the Bedminster Bridge is another footbridge, crossing from Clarence to York Road. Next comes the Bath Road Bridge which had a rather unhappy beginning.

Totterdown Lock seen from Temple Meads – the locks were filled in during the second world war to prevent the harbour being emptied by bombing

It collapsed under construction in 1806, was then rebuilt, only to be destroyed by a maverick barge in 1855. Beyond the present Bath Bridge, the third one to be built, stands the rather ugly tunnel of Temple Meads Station. At the exit of this tunnel we find ourselves at the end of the New Cut and back on the true course of the Avon, and yet another set of locks into the floating harbour. The Totterdown Locks were filled-in during the Second World War to prevent a direct hit from a bomb draining the harbour. These locks across the Feeder Road, follow the course taken by the Avon before the Cut was made.

The river then swings around under the steep hill of Totterdown, with its houses perched precariously on the top. Beneath Totterdown Bridge there are signs of ship-building, a slip where barges were built and repaired.

The Avon now journeys into a wilderness. The backs of trading estates and factories. It winds around St. Philips Marsh beneath the railway bridge of the now defunct Bristol to Wells line, then on to the bridge over the main London line at Netham. Here there is the tell-tale sign of a wharf, the remains of a dock wall that led into the back of Lysaghts Steel Works. Barges were loaded straight from the factory. To all intents and purposes, the tidal Avon ends here at the large 'V' shaped Netham Dam. High spring tides, during the equinoxes, push the tidal water up as far as Keynsham. Both the Netham Dam and the locks on the Feeder Canal ensure that the water in the floating harbour stays at a constant level.

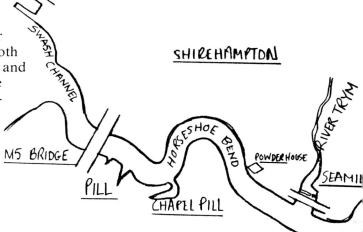

THE TIDAL AVON AND NEW CUT

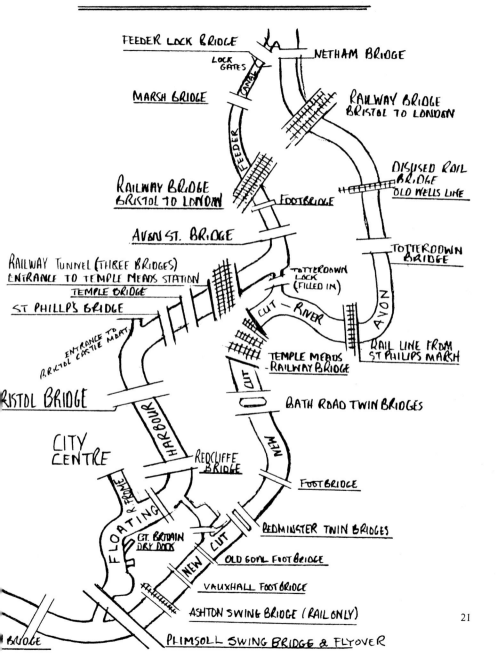

FEEDER LOCK BRIDGE

LOCK GATES

NETHAM BRIDGE

MARSH BRIDGE

RAILWAY BRIDGE
BRISTOL TO LONDON

FEEDER CANAL

DISUSED RAIL BRIDGE
OLD WELLS LINE

RAILWAY BRIDGE
BRISTOL TO LONDON

FOOTBRIDGE

AVON ST. BRIDGE

TOTTERDOWN
BRIDGE

RAILWAY TUNNEL (THREE BRIDGES)
ENTRANCE TO TEMPLE MEADS STATION

TOTTERDOWN
LOCK
(FILLED IN)

TEMPLE BRIDGE

ST PHILLP'S BRIDGE

CUT — RIVER

AVON

ENTRANCE TO
BRISTOL CASTLE MOAT

TEMPLE MEADS
- RAILWAY BRIDGE

RAIL LINE FROM
ST PHILIPS MARSH

BRISTOL BRIDGE

HARBOUR

CUT

BATH ROAD TWIN BRIDGES

CITY
CENTRE

NEW

REDCLIFFE
BRIDGE

FOOTBRIDGE

FLOATING R. FROME

GT. BRITAIN
DRY DOCK

NEW CUT

REDMINSTER TWIN BRIDGES

OLD GAOL FOOTBRIDGE

VAUXHALL FOOTBRIDGE

ASHTON SWING BRIDGE (RAIL ONLY)

BRIDGE

PLIMSOLL SWING BRIDGE & FLYOVER

21

The Floating Harbour

Beneath the "elegant piles" of Georgian Clifton the River Avon begins its course through the centre of Bristol. Matthew's guide of 1793 describes it as "Indubitably one of the most pleasant, healthy and elegant villages in the kingdom . . . commanding a pleasing prospect over one corner of the city and of vessels sailing up and down the Avon". With the exception of the vessels, Clifton is much the same today.

The merchants of Bristol made their money from the river and the western ocean beyond. During the 17th and 18th centuries many were 'privateers' (a polite name for pirates). The merchants then discovered slaving, the transporting of human cargo to the new colonies of the Americas. This they found to be both regular and profitable.

At the turn of the 18th century Bristol was a wealthy city. It then became fashionable – a spa no less. The hot wells of Hotwells, down by the muddy banks of the Avon, became a focal point for those very rich who wished to pamper themselves. That, of course, being only when no accommodation was available in Bath. Incredible claims were made of the Hotwells water, including *"curative effects for hot acrimonious blood, consumptions, stone and gravel, the stranguary, colliquative sweats, old diarrhoea, gout, gutache and the King's evil"*. However, as might have been expected, when the continent opened up at the end of the Napoleonic Wars, the rich deserted Hotwells. Afterwards, only the chronically sick came to Bristol's spa – to die!

Despite Bristol's popularity at the turn of the century, the docks themselves were in decline. Bristol was still a tidal port with particularly sharp rocks below the soft mud which were exposed at low tide. The famous saying "Ship Shape and Bristol Fashion" came about because a ship had to be well found in order to take the battering it received in the docks.

Between 1804 and 1809, the Bristol Port Authority engaged the engineer William Jessop to make Bristol docks into a floating harbour. Jessop built the Cumberland Basin. The South Lock, which is now permanently closed-off, is of special interest as it was rebuilt by Brunel in 1848 to allow more room for his ship, the Great Britain. The Brunel lock apart, Bristol's floating harbour is much the same as when Jessop completed it. In 1873 a new spur was added on the northern side of Cumberland Basin and locks were built to accommodate much larger vessels. This north entrance is now the only one into the harbour from the sea. Above the locks is the new swing bridge of the Cumberland Basin flyover complex. Nestling beneath this mighty structure on the north side is a small iron bridge, a relic of Isambard Kingdom Brunel's early engineering work. This was the very first use of wrought iron plates for bridge girders. The sister bridge now spanning the old Brunel lock is a copy and was built later, in 1872.

Leaving the Basin under the Junction Lock swing bridge, you pass the old pump house, built in Italianate style. It's engines supplied hydraulic power to lock gates, swing bridges and cranes in the dock and it is still pumping – these days draught beer! Also in the Junction Lock are the tidal or stop gates which are closed one and a half hours before high water on high spring tides to prevent tide water entering the dock.

Around the Hotwells area the river scene is rapidly changing from an industrial and commercial dock into a leisure and pleasure centre. The last remnants of cargo ships are the sand hoppers, disgorging their loads onto the dockside by the Mardyke.

On the site where Jessop built his dam across the original course of the Avon are the Port of Bristol workshops at Underfall Yard. It was originally named Overfall, as surplus water was released over the top. Unfortunately, this method caused serious silting in the dock. The Port Authority sought the advice of Brunel, who suggested the present underfall system – a culvert under the dam to dispose of the mud by a scouring action at ebb tide.

Beyond the Underfall Dam, where once stood huge timber yards, a leisure centre and new pub are to be found, which use the old May & Hassle office building. Alongside this is a wind-surfing school, complete with a new slipway, built for launching small boats.

During the early seventies, many Bristolians were worried about what might happen to the Avon waterway when the docks closed. There were even dark suggestions that much of the river would be decked-over and used as building land. There were protests, plans, more protests and more plans. While all this was going on, ignorant of what was happening, builders and owners of small craft were filling the docks, so that even before the decision was made to convert Bristol Docks into a marina, the harbour was crammed with people building and repairing boats, or just fiddling about on them.

Since that time most of the Port buildings, warehouses and land have taken on a new look. There is a new marina on Charles Hill's old slipway. On this historic site, new ships are taking shape in the form of steel fishing boats.

The Bristol Packet – a canal narrowboat setting off on a trip around Bristol Harbour

Other dock buildings have become the Great Britain Café and the tiny Brunel Buttery. In the larger sheds are an industrial museum, an arts centre, an exhibition centre and even a radio station. Others are used for the less glamorous purpose of storage.

Next to the former Charles Hill Shipyard is a dry dock which contains Brunel's iron ship, S.S. Great Britain. The ship was built in the very same dock and floated from it on 19th July 1843. The Great Britain was built by the Great Western Steamship Company and she epitomised the pride and audacity of her designer. Brunel had said of the Great Western Railway, "Why not make it longer and have a steamboat to go from Bristol to New York". It was this radical concept which led firstly to the building of the S.S. Great Western, a paddle steamer, and then, ten years later to the building of the iron, screw driven, S.S. Great Britain. She represented a giant step forward in ship design.

Charles Hill and Co. refused to build the new ship, so too did Patterson who had built the S.S. Great Western. The Great Western Steamship Company built their own dock in which to construct the S.S. Great Britain. The ship sailed many thousands of miles in service and finally ended her working life on the Australia run until in 1886, laden with coal, the ageing ship was unable to round Cape Horn. She found shelter in the Falkland Islands. There she remained for 84 years until, on 19th July 1970, she entered the dry dock where she had been built, having been towed the 8000 miles on a pontoon. She is at present being restored as a fitting memorial to her designer, I. K. Brunel.

The River Frome falls into the Avon in the centre of Bristol at St. Augustine's Reach. This is the site of the first major engineering work to be carried out on the Port of

The S.S. Great Britain in the dock where she was built

Bristol. A trench was cut to straighten out the Frome to a new junction downstream of Bristol Bridge. Previously, the course of the Frome had been roughly in line with Baldwin Street and joined the Avon by Bristol Bridge. The work was completed in 1248 and was a triumph of mediaeval engineering.

It's well known that John Cabot sailed from Bristol to discover Newfoundland. What is certainly not so well known is a story which surrounds Cabot and his historic journey to the New World. Cabot and his three sons, traders in Bristol, were asked by letter from the King to "seek out new lands", but he sent no money. However, he did send word to the Collector of Customs in Bristol to find twenty pounds from somewhere and to give it

GLEN AVON IN THE FLOATING HARBOUR.

to Cabot in return for a fifth of the profits (if any) from the voyage. The customs man duly conjured up the twenty pounds and passed it on to Cabot who then set sail. After fifty-four days sailing through storm and hardship they came to the New-found-land. This being a full year before Columbus landed on the American mainland. The international convention of that time stated that any newly discovered country should be named after the sponsor of the voyage and that only in the case of a monarch could the country take a christian name. It is now widely believed that America is named after the Italian navigator Amerigo Vespucci, but Amerigo is a christian name and Vespucci was no king, and anyway Cabot was there first. It could be that the continent was named after Cabot's sponsor, not the King, but the customs officer. His name was Richard Amerycke.

Moving upstream from St. Augustine's Reach, you pass under Prince Street swing bridge and on to the entrance to Bathurst Basin. The Basin itself has changed radically in the last few years, from a base for the Bristol sand trade to a secluded mooring for small boats. On the north side are some houses, some elegantly restored and some modern. The façade of an old warehouse in the Bristol Byzantine style has been thoughtfully included in the redevelopment of the area.

Beyond Bathurst Basin is the Redcliffe Bascule Bridge in the shadow of St. Mary Redcliffe. The straight beyond the bridge is called the Welsh Back and has more remains of that extraordinary architectural sub-style known as Bristol Byzantine – most notably in the shape of the Old Granary, now a music venue.

On then to Bristol Bridge and the heart of the old City of Bristol. There was a wooden bridge on the site in Saxon times which lasted until the Frome trench was built. The

Saxon bridge was replaced by one of stone, built on three massive piers, with houses on each side. It stood until 1768, when the present bridge was constructed.

Just beyond the bridge one striking piece of mediaeval Bristol is sadly missing. It would have risen from the banks of the Avon – It was Bristol Castle. "Sleighted", razed to the ground on Oliver Cromwell's orders after the Civil War, Bristol Castle was said to have been one of the largest and strongest in the country. It was built in the 13th century by Robert of Caen. Strangely, in spite of the plentiful supply of good building stone both in and around Bristol, Robert decided to ship all the stone from his home town of Caen in Normandy. It's possible that he felt the local pennant stone was too prone to splitting and weathering and that the Bath stone was too soft for a castle, or, perhaps he just happened to have shares in the Caen Stone firm. A few of the old quoines may still be seen from the river. The castle moat still exists and the opening can also be seen from the river. Its course is now underground and runs from a point opposite the corner of Courage Brewery, around to Wine Street, where it joins the underground course of the River Frome.

Travelling eastwards, you now pass under St. Philip's Bridge, once nicknamed Ha'penny Bridge. I thought this was because of the price of the toll but then discovered that one of the engineers on the docks reconstruction was named William Halfpenny. Most confusing. The present bridge replaced that damaged by bombing during the war. Between St. Philips and Temple Bridge which follows, rises a pencil-slim concrete tower, with an odd-looking control room affair on the top. This is the new lead shot tower, replacing the one, now sadly demolished, on Redcliffe Hill. It operates by allowing molten lead to fall through a kind of collander. As the droplets fall they solidify and land at the bottom as perfect spheres of lead.

Bathurst Basin and the Ostrich Inn

Under Temple Bridge and just visible on the north bank is yet another piece of Bristol Byzantine, Gardiner & Son, said to be inspired by the Uffitzi Palace. This is all that remains of a long line of Bristol Soap Boilers. This rather fanciful factory once manufactured the famous "Puritan" soap.

A little further on are the three bridges of the Temple Meads railway station approach, which combine to make a tunnel. The centre section was part of Brunel's Paddington to Bristol line, the remaining two being constructed later, as increased rail traffic came to Bristol.

Beyond the railway bridge is the Feeder Canal and the sealed-off locks at Totterdown Basin where the Avon rejoins the New Cut. Now much overgrown after a partial

Entrance to Bristol Castle Moat opposite Courage brewery

An example of Bristol Byzantine architecture – 'Puritan' soap was once made in this building

restoration a few years ago, the Feeder Canal runs past the 'backs' of industrial Bristol. Grey factories, some with a rather oddly placed Gothick splendour.

At Barton Hill the scene alters slightly, most industrial buildings having now been demolished, including (as this is written) the remains of the Blackswarth lead and copper smelting factories with their clinker-topped walls.

The Netham Lock ensures that the floating harbour stays at a constant level. At high spring tides the locks are closed to prevent water entering from up river. They are also closed during flood conditions upstream of the dock. At Netham Lock the full circle of river and floating harbour converges.

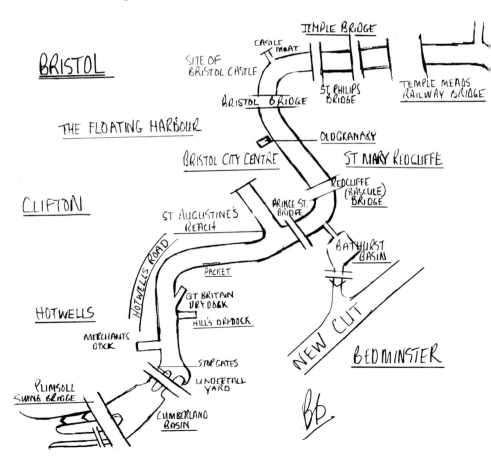

Avon Navigation

Beyond the lock and weir at Netham the city is left behind, but not the industrial sites. During the 18th, 19th and 20th centuries heavy industry stayed close to the Avon, which was used as an open sewer, carrying the toxic wastes of the lead and copper smelters. These industries are now very much extinct, including the St. Anne's Board Mills, a very recent loss.

Crews Hole, further up river, was once an intensive industrial area, consisting of smoking, stinking and polluting foundries, coal mines and chemical factories. Unlike a number of the Bristol factories which did manage to have some regard for workers and environment, the Crews Hole works were described thus:– *"Here there are no palatial buildings, nothing of the aesthetic, and sentiment is altogether absent. It is no more than a hard, grimy business."* Mercifully, on most days of the year, Crews Hole was downwind of Bristol!

The last, large industrial complex at Crews Hole is the site of a further tar distillery. Tar is a by-product of coal and at first it was simply nasty black stuff that nobody wanted. That was until the chemists got hold of it. In 1819, one of these men, a Scot, found that one of the by-products of tar was a solvent for rubber. He rubberised fabrics, making them waterproof. His name was Macintosh!

One more by-product of tar is creosote. It was patented in 1838 and came to the attention of Mr. I. K. Brunel who needed preservatives for the sleepers and bridge building materials on his Bristol to Exeter railway – and that's how the Crews Hole distillery came to be built. During 1981/82 (between filming and the writing of this book) the tar distillery was flattened to make way for a "leisure park". All that is left of the industrial past are the remains of the engine house of the Crews Hole coal pit, and at the top of Troopers' Hill, above Crews Hole, stands a rather forlorn chimney. It was built to take away some of the more toxic smoke from the valley below, but has not smoked now for over seventy years.

Beyond Crews Hole lies Conham Vale and here the Avon changes character, pastoral, it flows between tree-lined banks towards Hanham, although even here there are tell-tale signs of 18th and 19th century toil. The slag heap of Hanham coal mine shows just above the tree line. A round-topped hill. Also at regular intervals along this route the bare rock face reveals the site of quarries, where pennant sandstone was hewn for building work in the region.

The south bank, at St. Annes, is steep-sided and wooded. At the bottom nestles the Ariel Rowing Club boathouse, which, on hot summer days, can evoke that nostalgic Edwardian vision of endless sunshine, straw boaters and cucumber sandwiches.

The idyllic peace is shattered at regular intervals by trains emerging from St. Anne's railway tunnel. From the north bank Brunel's fine railway plays hide and seek as it hugs the course of the Avon towards Bath, trains dashing through tunnels and cuttings and making sudden noisy appearances along the way.

Also at St. Annes is Beezes Tea Gardens, which I remember so well from my childhood. It's still much the same. The ferry transports people to and from the north bank. Now fully licensed, the gardens offer more than just tea. They also run river trips in "The Princess Anne" pleasure boat. These summer trips are usually rounded-off in the evenings by a barbeque at the gardens.

Perhaps the nicest way to see this stretch of the Avon is to take the towpath from Netham Lock to Hanham. This path takes the right or north bank all the way – in river navigation the right bank is on the right hand when proceeding downstream.

At Hanham Lock the River Avon leaves the jurisdiction of the Port of Bristol and becomes the concern of the British Waterways Board. Here at Hanham, you come to the first weir on the river. Weirs closed the Avon to navigation some time in the 13th century. This was a direct result of the Bristol guild system, a closed shop policy run by Bristol so that only Bristolians could run the mills. Disgruntled millers moved away from the city and constructed their mills on the Avon and its tributaries.

The Avon was closed to navigation upstream from Hanham for nearly five hundred years. In Elizabethan times several schemes were suggested to link the Avon with the Thames, although none of these came to fruition. However, in 1712 a bill was passed for the purpose of "*clearing, making and effecting a passage for boats and other vessels upon the River Avon.*" This bill led to the construction of Hanham Lock, which was actually the beginning of the Kennet and Avon Canal.

By 1740 the river was navigable up to Bath. Trade was brisk and passengers were also carried for one shilling a trip, which took four hours. The Chequers Inn at Hanham was obviously a port-of-call for both the bargees and their passengers. Behind the Inn was once a cock pit, where men from the barges and quarries enjoyed the sport

of cock-fighting, although this pastime more usually ended in a brawl as precious wages were gambled away.

The one and three quarter miles from Hanham Lock to Keynsham Lock is dominated by the Fry's "Garden Factory", built in the twenties. It represents a kind of buccolic, capitalist dream. Somerdale, where contented workers, in beautiful surroundings, produce sweet things to eat. It is probably the least offensive factory building alongside the Avon.

The Chequers Inn at Hanham from the Keynsham Bank

Ariel Rowing Club
St Annes

Further upstream on the north bank, an arched bridge stands over Siston Brook where it enters the Avon, and alongside, a disused, stone built wharf, known as the Londonderry Coal Wharf. Here horse-drawn trams brought the coal from the mines at Warmley and Mangotsfield, where it was loaded into barges for transport elsewhere. The weigh house still stands on the line of the tramway, which was a branch of the Avon & Gloucestershire Railway, whose other tramline into Bristol became the Midland Railway line from Temple Meads to Mangotsfield.

At Keynsham Lock a rise of 2.33 metres or 7 feet 8 inches takes the Avon out of the tidal influence. Exceptionally high tides come up to Keynsham and when these coincide with heavy rainfall it can spell disaster, as in 1968 when the County Bridge was swept away. Here, the River Chew falls into the Avon and the remains of yet another brass mill can be seen, recognisable by the distinctive cupola on top of the clock tower. This mill was once worked by a partnership which included Abraham Darby who, when he failed to interest his partners in his new iron process, (that of using coke instead of charcoal), moved to Coalbrookdale. It is interesting to try and envisage how Keynsham and its environs might appear today had Darby not made his move.

Beyond Keynsham Lock is the White Hart bridge, a typical stone canal bridge. The hostelry from which it gets its name is alongside the lock cutting. It is now called, incredibly, Isle d'Avon! The inn was used as a guard post during both the Civil War and the Monmouth Rebellion.

Leaving Keynsham, at the end of the lock cutting is the entrance to Portavon Marina, with its facilities for mooring and repairs. On the opposite bank, more industry; a paper mill followed by a trading estate, and

Swinford copper mills – the mill stream

back on the north bank are the remains of another coal wharf, at the end of another defunct tramline.

At Bitton, the River Boyd joins the Avon and at this point the river is crossed by the Ferris Horsebridge. This bridge allowed horses (towing barges) to cross the Boyd. A little further on a railway bridge crosses the river. This is part of the now closed section of the Midland Region railway line from Bristol to Bath. It is now a cycle track which runs from Bitton station to Bath.

The next weir on the river is at Swinford, the site of another copper mill. The lock is on the south bank and the weir sweeps across towards the mill, which is still in use as a factory, but no longer uses water power from the mill wheels.

For those who do not travel the river by boat, Swinford locks are the most secluded and perhaps the most mysterious since they cannot be reached by road and, unlike any other lock between Bristol and Bath, there is no public house nearby.

From Swinford to Saltford is a mere twelve hundred yards. Here again we see signs of copper mills. The mills on the north bank at Kelston are the most impressive since the annealing furnaces are still standing. These mills and the others at Saltford would, in the nineteenth century, have belched smoke, fumes and polluting waste into the Avon Valley. Happily, things are different nowadays.

Alongside Saltford Lock stands the Jolly Sailor, ready to furnish the ravenous traveller with good ale and food in the pub garden beside the lock. At weekends an amazing sight is to be seen as dozens of dinghies from the Bristol Avon Sailing Club gather en masse in the straight just beyond the lock gate.

The Locks on the Avon at Twerton in Bath

Another short trip to Kelston Lock finds the Saltford Marina on the south bank, together with yet another brass mill, with the lock on the north, or Kelston, side. (This lock is often mistakenly referred to as the Saltford Lock . . . the Saltford Lock is at Kelston, on the Saltford side). Beyond the lock runs the longest straight reach on the river, a mile or so in length. Around the next bend the cycle track railway again passes over the river.

Newbridge is the gateway to the City of Bath. Built of Bath stone, its exceptionally graceful arch is an appetiser for the many architectural delights to come. Beneath Newbridge, skiffs may be hired from Cox's Boating Services, to row upon the river – downstream traffic only.

Approaching Bath, the river flows along the inevitable "backs" of industrial developments, and passes the work-a-day side of the City, that part normally unseen by tourists. At Twerton, the last lock of the original Avon Navigation Bill rises 14 ft. to take the river 42 ft. above the first lock at Hanham. At Twerton Lock there is no picturesque weir, but instead a series of automatic sluices – all part of the essential Bath flood prevention scheme. The cutting beyond the Twerton Lock is the longest on the Avon. At the beginning there is a minute bridge which almost hides the pub from which it gets its name – The Dolphin. This is a canal pub and proud of it, with its front door opening on to the cutting and the back door onto the road.

Beyond the cutting are more factories and an assortment of bridges, the most noteworthy being the Victoria Suspension Bridge, tucked away between two factories, and now used by pedestrians only. This bridge was opened in 1836. Its suspension rods are inclined outwards towards the piers instead of being vertical. Where the bridge crosses the river the old railway cycle track comes

The most elegant bridge on the Avon, Pulteney Bridge at Bath

to an end. A good way for walkers to see the river is to take the towpath on the north bank into the centre of Bath.

Bath, Spa, Roman City, Georgian City, owes it fame not to the waters of the Avon but to those of the hot springs. Their powers of healing go back well before the Romans. Around 500 B.C., Bladud, a young West Country prince, was found to be suffering from a form of leprosy, and was exiled from the court. Poor Bladud finished up tending pigs who then also began to show signs of the disease. The pigs came to wallow in the mud surrounding the hot springs of Bath, and miraculously their sores began to disappear. Bladud bathed in the mud and he too was cured. He became king and Bath became a sacred place of healing.

Since Elizabethan times, the City of Bath had petitioned for a navigable river from Avonmouth to Bath. When the city was enjoying a popular revival under Master of Ceremonies, Beau Nash, the citizens again presented a bill, claiming that: "Great difficulty was being experienced in getting materials for the new buildings of Georgian Bath". The Bill was defeated. In 1724 a deed assigned the river to the Duke of Beaufort and others, called the Proprietors of Navigation between Bath and Hanham Mills. This made it possible to canalise the Avon and work began immediately.

The first barge arrived on the 15th December, 1727, carrying "Deal boards, pig lead and meal". So, if a waterway to Bath, why not to London? The obvious course was to continue up the Avon, locking each weir to the furthest point east. Then drive a canal through to the Thames. Ferdinando Stratford surveyed the river and pronounced the route to be a possibility, but nothing was done. Dreams of a waterway to the capital only became a

The Kennet and Avon Canal above Widcombe in Bath

reality with the formation of the Kennet & Avon Canal Company.

At Churchill Bridge, the towpath changes banks, passing beneath Mr. Brunel's railway and on to lock No. 7, Widcombe Lock. This lock is the continuation of the Kennet and Avon navigation to London. The locks rise steeply, taking the canal high above the river. The sterling work carried out by the Kennet and Avon Canal Trust will make navigation as far as Devizes possible by 1985.

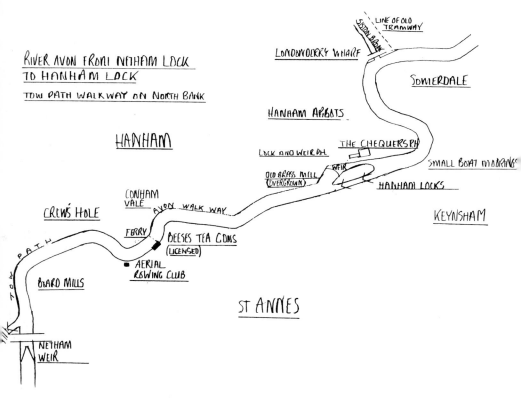

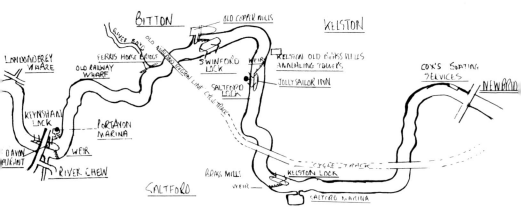

Back to the river and the beauty of Pulteney Bridge, undoubtedly the most elegant across the Avon. The sweep of the three-stepped weir provides a unique setting for the bridge, surrounded by honey coloured Bath stone mansions. It was designed by Robert Adam and opened in 1770. Pulteney is one of only three bridges left in the world with shops and buildings on the bridge span itself. There are no locks at Pulteney Weir, so navigation by small craft ends here.

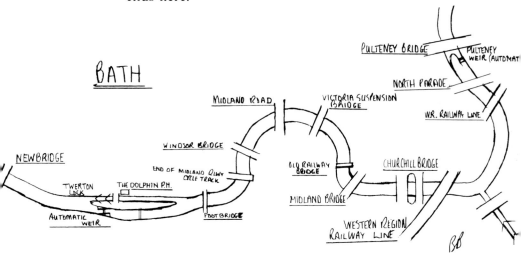

Towards The Source

If the southern aspect of Pulteney Bridge is all elegance and beauty, then the same cannot be said of the northern side. In contrast, the river here is flanked by flat walls of old and modern buildings and yet more factory backs, until reaching the Cleveland Bridge, opened in 1827, the first steel bridge in the city of stone.

A mile or so upstream lies Bathampton, whose weir once served two mills. A small bridge spans the river here, sharing with the mighty Suspension Bridge, the distinction of being the only other toll bridge on the River Avon.

Above Bathampton the character of the river changes slightly, being shallower and running a little faster. The Avon takes the water of St. Catherine's and Bye Brook before reaching a bend which takes you south into the most beautiful stretch of the river. Like the Bristol Avon Gorge, it is an Ice Age valley, just as high, but less dramatic, with smooth, wooded hillsides and verdant slopes. Standing sentinel at the Bath end of the valley is Brown's Folly, a square tower, built by local quarry owner Wade Brown in 1840. Quarrying is another link with the Bristol Gorge but here, instead of slicing off the sides of the hill, Bath stone was mined from underneath the hills.

Passing the Folly, the river, the Kennet & Avon canal, the railway line to Westbury and the A36 road all squeeze together forming a kind of chicane in the neck of the valley.

Quiet section of the Kennet and Avon Canal near Claverton

In the last century there was another railway, one that came down from the side of the valley, bringing the quarry stone to be loaded into barges on the canal. This was at Bathampton Tramway and some of the stone sleepers still remain.

High above the river stands Claverton Manor, one time home of Ralph Allen, a famous citizen of Bath. This man made two fortunes, one from the cross-posts, a kind of provincial postal service, and the other from the stone quarries above Bath. Allen provided much of the stone for John Wood to rebuild Bath in all its glory. He bought Claverton Manor in 1758, rebuilt in its present neo-Grecian style in 1820. Nowadays it is a museum, an American museum. Allen also had a hand in the fledgling canal company.

Also at Claverton is the pumping station, where water was raised from the Avon to the canal, using the power of the river. Two water wheels worked a pair of beam-pumps which pushed the water up to the canal.

The Kennet & Avon enjoyed nearly forty years of prosperity, from 1810 until 1849. The journey from Bristol to London took five days and a barge carrying 60 tons of South Wales coal could reach London within a week. A sedate pace, but quiet and reliable.

Then came the railways. With the opening of Mr. Brunel's line from London to Bristol in 1841, the G.W.R. undercut the canal transport prices. Finally the end was in sight and the canal company sold out to the Great Western who, not unnaturally, allowed the canal to run down, in spite of their assurances to the contrary. By 1910 commercial traffic on the canal had virtually ceased. However, after a long period of restoration by the Canal Trust, the section from Bath to Dundas Aqueduct was reopened in 1982.

The Dundas Aqueduct

As the canal swaps banks with the river, the Avon flows under Dundas Aqueduct. This splendid construction is named after one of the founders of the Canal Company, Admiral Dundas.

At Dundas stand the remains of an even more bewildering feat of engineering. At the turn of the eighteenth century work commenced on the Somerset Coal Canal, a branch line of the Kennet & Avon, to enable coal from the Radstock and Midsomer Norton mines to be transported to the river ready for shipment. To construct a waterway across the Mendips was a daunting task. Several new innovations were tried, such as caisson lifts and an incline for the barges, but these were eventually abandoned in favour of conventional locks. The final obstacle, a sudden drop of 130 ft. from Combe Hay to Dundas Aqueduct, contained a flight of 22 locks. The work was completed in 1805 and the remains of the Combe Hay locks are in remarkably good condition considering they have not been used for 80 years.

Beyond Dundas, the river and canal run parallel. The Midford Brook joins the Avon at Limpley Stoke. This brook runs under the splendid Midford Road Viaduct. Also at Limpley Stoke stands another weir and mill. The river now takes on the appearance of a stream. The water is clearer and weeds wave in the shallows.

The Avon then flows through the village of Freshford, a conservation area, and is joined by the River Frome. Beyond this point the River Avon leaves the new county which uses its name, and from here to the source it is now flowing through Wiltshire, a proper county!

The river is followed by both the canal and railway. The canal recrosses the Avon at the Avoncliffe Aqueduct, another monument to landscape architecture. A short distance from here the canal and river part company, while the river pursues the course made by nature, the canal takes the carefully surveyed route across the backbone of the country to the River Kennet in Berkshire, and from there into the Thames and London.

At Bradford-on-Avon a footbridge crosses the river to the old tithe barn. Both were built in the 14th century. Undoubtedly the town's most interesting building is the Saxon church of St. Lawrence, founded in the 7th century. Bradford-on-Avon is a beautiful town, where houses and factories cascade down the hill towards the river. Bradford is in the manufacturing business, yet the factories manage to blend perfectly with the other buildings. At the riverside, old mills have been restored by the Avon Rubber Company. At the centre of the town is the Bradford-on-Avon Bridge with its old lock-up gaol, some 250 years old. Like many other towns on the Avon, Bradford was built on the wool trade. Its prosperity lasted for centuries, until the Napoleonic Wars caused a massive recession. Until the coming of the canal and railway, Bradford was bankrupt.

Twin Bridges over the Avon at Lacock. The further bridge is over dry land awaiting inevitable flooding

Out of Bradford, the Avon seems to be making for Trowbridge, but then makes a little wiggle, pausing only to take water from the River Biss. It then turns north east to Staverton, and an old cloth mill where today the Nestlé Company has taken over. This old mill was once twice the size until one bonfire night in the 1890's when the factory mysteriously burnt down. It was rebuilt, but only to half its original height.

As the Avon runs through Wiltshire, it is a story of flooding, flooding and more flooding. Only one heavy rainstorm is needed for the river to start rising rapidly. At Melksham there are more automatic flood gates to check the water.

At Lacock, one of two bridges stands on dry land awaiting flood waters. Lacock is a National Trust village, also built on the cloth trade; the Avon, until the 12th century, was used to transport wool "giving access to the sea at Avonmouth".

The Avon passes Lacock Abbey, previously the home of the inventor of photography, Fox Talbot. A story connected with the Abbey is that of Olive Sharrington, daughter of the owner of Lacock, who, against her parents' wishes, became betrothed to John Talbot. Despairing of ever marrying him, she lept from the Abbey battlements. Her petticoats billowed and slowed her descent. The poor girl then landed on her lover. They both recovered and later married. Olive's father said, *"Since she has made such leaps, she should e'en marry him"*. A fatherly blessing.

Chippenham is a Saxon name meaning, roughly, "market town on a river loop". It is perhaps worth asking why, back in the canal building days, the Avon was not made navigable as far as Chippenham, some fifteen miles nearer

Maud Heath's causeway

to London. A large saving might well have been made on canal construction costs.

In Mediaeval times both flooding and its slippery, slimy aftermath, made reaching the market at Chippenham a rather gruelling affair. In 1474 Maud Heath made a bequest of land to build and maintain a causeway, or raised path, through the swamp to Chippenham market. The causeway was duly built and can still be seen today near the banks of the Avon at Kellaways between Chippenham and Calne.

Heading towards its source, the river now becomes quite fast flowing in parts. It passes close to the villages of Sutton Benger and Christian Malford, then on under the M4 motorway with its "River Avon" sign.

At Dauntsey the Avon reaches its furthest point east and here turns northwards towards Great Somerford. From Great Somerford until Malmesbury the river runs across farmland. Tall reeds on its banks provide cover for water-fowl. Sadly, this rather beautiful stretch is on private land, and, therefore rather difficult to reach. The river is seen again from the bridge which takes the Malmesbury to Swindon road. Here it runs over shallows with trout in abundance.

At Malmesbury another Avon falls quietly and un-obstrusively into the Bristol Avon. This is the Tetbury Avon. On the high ridge between these two rivers sits Malmesbury. The town of Malmesbury had seven mills, weaving first cloth and then silk, making it famous throughout Europe until, at the end of the 19th century, trade ceased to flourish. Like many other towns along the Avon, Malmesbury bears a resemblance to one of the Italian or Provençal hilltowns, with their narrow lanes, steps and an air of privacy surrounding each plot.

The town is dominated by its Abbey and in the year 1010 a monk, named Elmer, made for himself a pair of wings and attempted to fly from the Abbey tower. He did, in fact, fly nearly 60 feet, in the manner of a brick, to the bottom, and was crippled for the remainder of his life.

From Malmesbury the river follows the Sherston Road. It has become both narrower and shallower and the source is now to the west.

Near Easton Grey, a magnificent and immaculately maintained village, the Avon is crossed by the Fosseway, the Roman road which runs from Devon to Lincolnshire. The crossing point is now marked by a small, stone bridge.

The furthest point east – the bridge over the Avon at Dauntsey

At Sherston the Avon is no more than a brook. Here again the stream of water divides, coming partly from the direction of Luckington and partly from Sopworth. Information on the source of the Avon is also divided. Some books name Luckington and others Sopworth. The Wessex Water Authority is unsure!

The Luckington source emerges at a well, near the ruins of an old slaughterhouse to the west of the village. A dry stream bed continues under the bridge which crosses the Chipping Sodbury to Malmesbury road.

The Sopworth source is Crow Down Springs. It can be found in a field shortly beyond a small hump-backed bridge on the Sopworth/Luckington road.

The Tetbury Avon is the third contender, rising next to the Tetbury sewage works.

The true source, it seems, cannot be determined until a complete hydrological survey of the area has been carried out. The deepest will be the winner.

Covering 75 miles, the Bristol Avon is one of Britain's longest rivers and only on the Avon is it possible, in good visibility, to view the mouth only a mile or so from the source.

Going to the source of the Avon is not quite the "Search for the Nile", more of a mini adventure, but one that I found interesting and enjoyable and most of all satisfying. To be able to say, *"well that's it, now I've seen the source, now I know"*. Except, of course, in the end I discovered that there were three sources!

What mystery to solve now? The Malago which runs through darkest Bedminster, or the Bye Brook or perhaps the Severn Thames Canal? Who knows?

The Avon near the Luckington Source

A mere trickle under a bridge near the Sopworth Source, Crow Down Springs

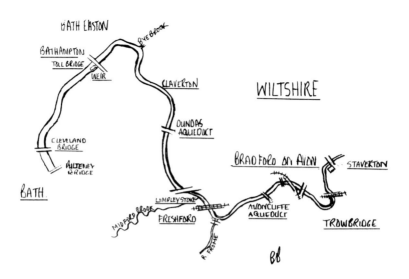

Bibliography

Bryan Little, *Portrait of Somerset* (Robert Hale Ltd. 1969)

R. A. Buchanan & Neil Cossons, *The Industrial Archaeology of the Bristol Region* (David & Charles 1969)

L. T. C. Rolt, *Isambard Kingdom Brunel* (Longmans 1957)

Peter J. Stuckey, *The Sailing Pilots of the Bristol Channel* (David & Charles 1977)

Arthur Mee, *The King's England. Somerset* (Hodder & Stoughton 1968)

Arthur Mee, *The King's England. Gloucestershire* (Hodder & Stoughton 1966)

Arthur Mee, *The King's England. Wiltshire* (Hodder & Stoughton 1962)

John Haddon, *Portrait of Avon* (Robert Hale Ltd. 1981)

Kenneth R. Clew, *The Kennet & Avon Canal* (David & Charles 1968)

Derrick Becket, *Brunel's Britain* (David & Charles 1980)

Bristol Avon River Authority Survey of Water Resources (March 1973)

J. M. Willoughby, *The Bristol Avon Hanham Lock to Bath*

Diana Winsor, *Dream of Bath* (Trade & Travel 1980)

Bob Baker was born in St. George, Bristol in 1939. His childhood haunts were around the River Avon at Crews Hole and Conham Vale. He graduated from Air Balloon Hill Junior School to Air Balloon Hill Secondary Modern at the age of eleven. On finishing his secondary education at fifteen, he joined the Bristol Co-operative Society as an apprentice stone mason (monumental). It was here that his writing career began in earnest with hammer and chisel. At 21 he became a student at the West of England College of Art and left holding a National Diploma in Design, plus strong interest in animated film. It was this that led him over the next five years to become involved in film and TV writing.

He started writing in 1968 in partnership with David Martin. They wrote for many well known TV series such as 'Dr. Who', 'Z Cars', 'Public Eye', 'Target' and others. He and David Martin also wrote many original plays and serials, notably 'Thick As Thieves', which won a British Television Society award, 'The Pye Oscar'. Since the partnership ended in 1979, Bob Baker has been Story Editor on the first series of 'Shoestring' and has since been working at HTV and has written and helped create new series such as 'Into The Labyrinth' and more recently the highly praised 'Jangles', and of course the documentary which is the subject of this his first book.

The Town Bridge.
Bradford on Avon